Dot to Dot

Books For Kids

Fun Animal Coloring and Connect the Dot Books for Kids Ages 4 - 8

DOT TO DOT BOOKS FOR KIDS

DOT TO DOT BOOKS FOR KIDS IS PERFECT FOR HOME SCHOOL AND PRESCHOOL FOR YOUNG CHILDREN. THIS WORKBOOK WILL HELP YOUR CHILD PRACTICE COUNTING NUMBERS AND DEVELOP THE FINE MOTOR CONTROL THEY NEED FOR THE FUTURE WHILE THEY CONNECT THE DOTS AND COLOR THESE FUN COLORING ANIMAL FILLED PAGES.

WHAT'S INSIDE:

- SINGLE SIDED COLORING PAGES TO PREVENT BLEED THROUGH OF COLOR TO ADDITIONAL PAGES

- LARGE 8 X 10 INCH PAGES

- FUN ANIMAL COLORING PAGES AND DOT TO DOT ACTIVITIES

- EACH DOT TO DOT PUZZLE HAS A RANGE BETWEEN 20 – 60 DOTS PER PUZZLE.

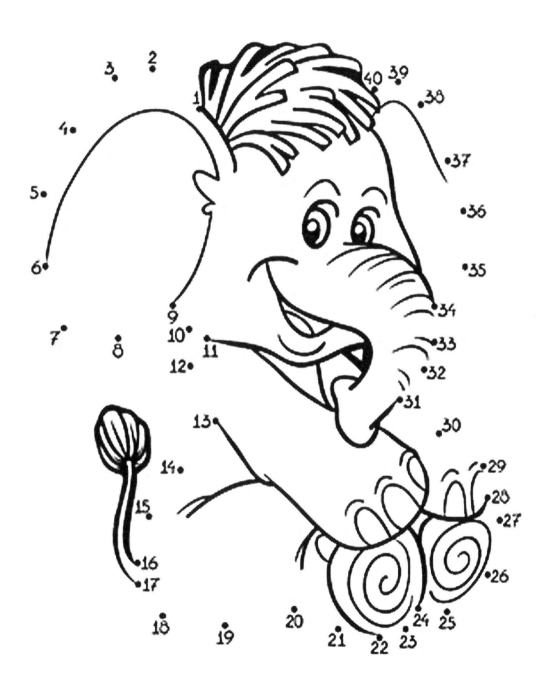

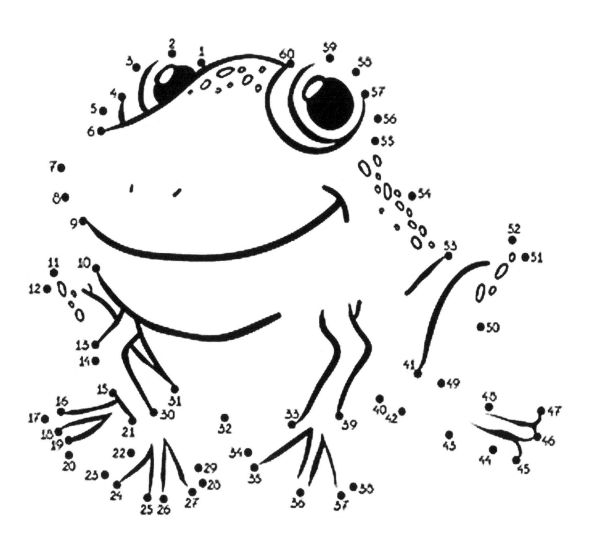

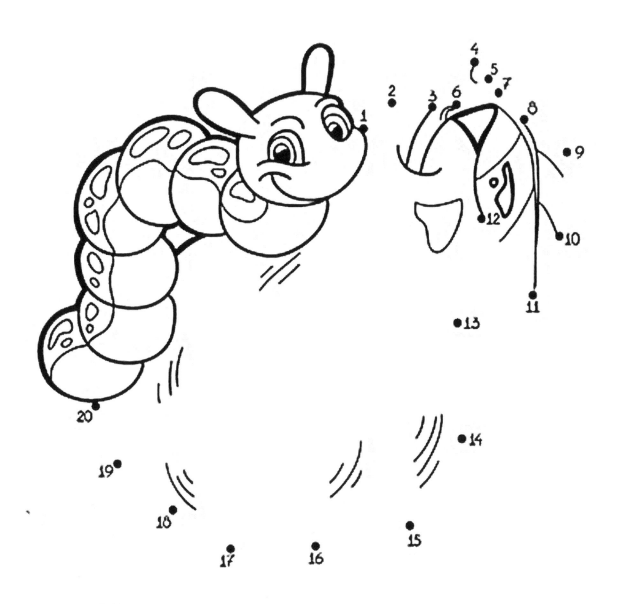

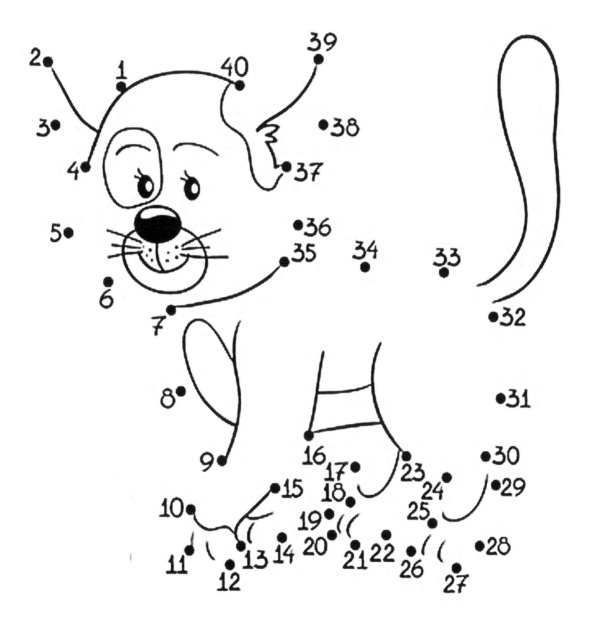

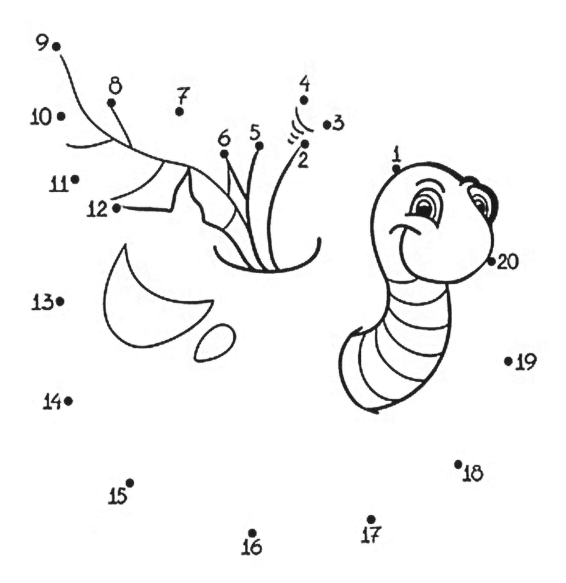

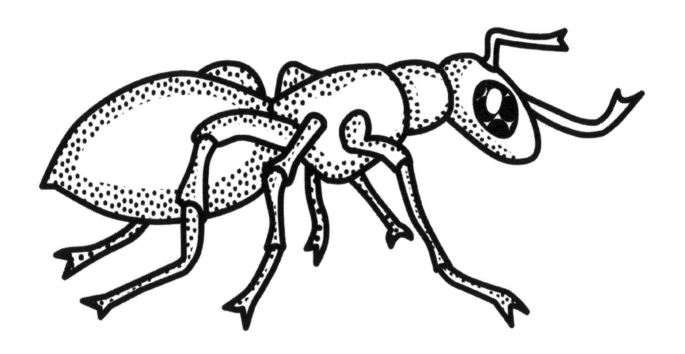

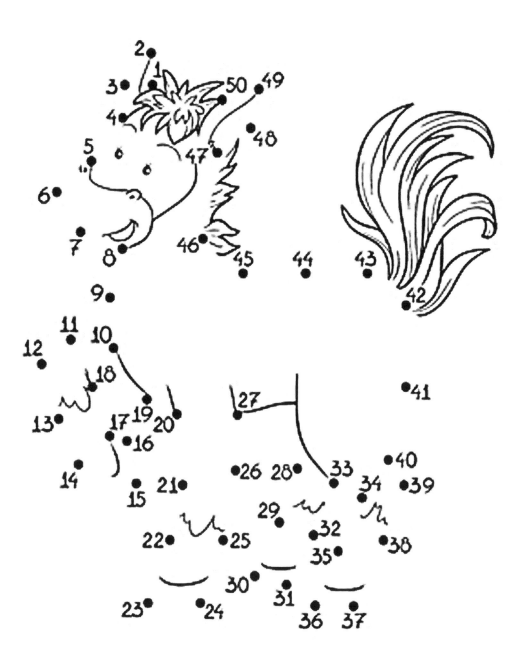

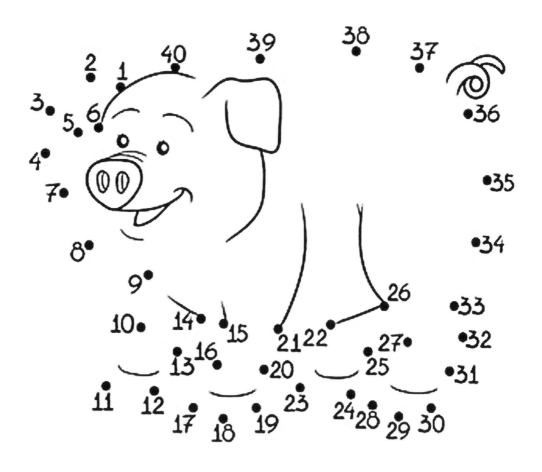

Made in the USA
Las Vegas, NV
01 December 2020